MW01067873

Irish Wolfhound From Puppy to Adult

A Basic Guide to Understanding This Giant Breed

By

L.A. Marie

Copyright © 2015 L.A. Marie

All rights reserved.

ISBN 10 1512077321

ISBN 13 9781512077322

Psalm 104

5-30

1

This book is dedicated to anyone who has ever had their heart stolen by the magnificent and noble breed, the Irish Wolfhound.

Contents

Chapter 11: Have Fun with Your Hound

Chapter One
Is the Irish Wolfhound Right For Me?

Introduction

So you're thinking about adopting an Irish Wolfhound. Congratulations! Nothing is more rewarding than having your faithful, loving friend at your side. A companion who won't judge you based on what you look like, what you do for a living, how you dress, or if you combed your hair this morning. A best buddy who loves to be in your company, whether you're navigating a rugged mountain trail, taking a stroll around the neighborhood, or just hanging out in front of the television. The Irish Wolfhound (or IW) can pretty much do it all. However, to be fair to both you and the dog, there are some things to consider *before* you bring one of these noble animals into your family.

Let's begin by taking a look at some of the pros and cons of being a proud IW owner, and the characteristics of this ancient and majestic dog. Keep in mind that as with any breed, they are individuals. Though most well-bred and socialized animals will exhibit the traits that are typical of the IW, there are occasionally animals that will deviate from the norm.

Pros and Cons

Pros:
- Tallest of all the dog breeds (Can also be a con depending on your point of view)
- People orientated—make great family dogs
- Good with children
- Gentle, patient, easy going disposition

- Gets along with other dogs and pets if properly socialized
- Intelligent
- Easy to train
- Loyal to their family
- Are often couch potatoes in the house despite their size
- Does not generally require a great deal of time to groom

Cons:
- Tallest of all the dog breeds (Can also be a pro depending on your point of view)
- Require bigger everything: bed, x-pen, space in car, size appropriate toys, etc.
- Veterinary maintenance is more expensive
- Will chase prey—use caution when you allow off-leash
- Doesn't tolerate heat well—prefers cooler weather
- Shorter life span than some other breeds
- Somewhat expensive to purchase quality dog
- Harder to restrain—must teach obedience from a young age

Now that we have a basic understanding of what to expect from an Irish Wolfhound, it's time to take a closer look to make sure they will fit into the lifestyle of your family. After all, a Pekinese wouldn't be well suited for a runner looking for a jogging companion, just as an IW wouldn't be a good choice for someone who wants a small lap dog. Still, the Irish Wolfhound would certainly try to fit in your lap given the opportunity.

A Closer Look at the Irish Wolfhound

The Irish Wolfhound wins the crown as the world's tallest breed, yet they are not the heaviest. Although you might beg to differ when they step on your foot, which is a commonplace occurrence. By the time they reach eighteen months of age, the minimum height and weight standard for a male is 32 inches at the shoulder (or withers) and 120 pounds, whereas the minimum height and weight for a female is 30 inches and 105 pounds. Keep in mind this is the minimum, as many hounds will reach sizes greater than that. Yet despite their enormous size, they will frequently try to push into tight spaces and don't understand why your little ten pound Fido fits in your lap and they don't. That's not for a lack of trying though.

For many, their height is both a pro and a con depending on the situation. It's nice to be able to pet your pal without having to do deep knee bends, but these dogs are excellent counter surfers. They would be all too happy to snack on the defrosting New York steak that's sitting by the kitchen sink. Just because you left something on the counter doesn't make it safe. Their reach is deceptive. Early training for this breed—and frankly for any breed in my opinion—is a must. But we'll talk more about training later.

One of the IW's best traits is that they are very people orientated. They adore their family and want nothing more than to spend time with you. Whether that means going for a walk, supervising as you do your chores, or simply hanging out by your feet while you watch your favorite flick on T.V., you'll find your faithful hound at your side. (Or in front of you, or behind you, or best yet, leaning up against you.) If you're looking for a dog that you can play with five minutes a day, then toss out and ignore the rest of the time, then stop right now. The Irish Wolfhound is not for you. Do yourself a favor and find a breed that isn't as attached to people, or better yet, reconsider the reasons you want a dog in the first place. However, if you want a companion to share your home and your life with, then the Irish Wolfhound definitely fits the bill.

That's not to say your IW can't ever be left alone, because that's certainly not the case. These dogs were bred to be independent thinkers, and are quite happy spending time outside watching over their kingdom—otherwise known as the backyard. Yet in order to be content, they need to be **a part** of the family, not **apart** from the family.

Trustworthy, loyal, and dependable, the IW is also a wonderful choice if you have kids because these dogs tend to be very gentle and patient. You also don't have to be as concerned with the child hurting the dog like you would a Chihuahua or other small breed. Just be cautious because the IW does grow quickly, and can accidently knock over young Jack or Jill without meaning to. Young hounds in particular are a bit on the clumsy side. Yet regardless of their giant stature, they are **not** a horse. This is a running breed, not a draft breed. You can seriously injure your hound if you allow your children to try to ride him (or her). They are also not built to pull wagons or drag other objects. Leave that to the draft breeds. Nevertheless, it is safe for them to carry their own backpacks on hikes as long as the packs are not overloaded, and you do not ask the dog to work at too young an age.

Generally speaking, the IW gets along well with other dogs. However I must strongly advise you to introduce your hound—preferably as a puppy—to your small dogs carefully and teach them little Fido isn't a chew toy. My hounds live with tiny dogs as small as six pounds without any issues, but caution is certainly advised. Your hound needs to know Fido is one of the pack, not prey. Be aware that the hound could accidently injure a small animal if the play gets too rough.

Another factor to consider before adopting an IW is that they are sighthounds. This means they were bred to hunt their prey primarily by sight and speed rather than scent, and that instinct is still very strong. So if they see Peter Cottontail hopping down the bunny trail, you can bet your dog will give chase, and since they are a galloping hound, they are incredibly fast. Once they lock onto their target, it can be difficult if not impossible to get them to stop. Consideration must be taken before allowing your IW off-leash. There are many potential dangers for your dog if he takes off at thirty plus miles per hour and runs into a street, barrels headfirst into a wire fence, runs onto a rancher's private property where he could be shot, or a multitude of other unforeseen hazards.

You must also realize that cats and other small dogs can be mistaken as prey, especially in the wrong environment. As stated above, this is not to say that IW's don't get along well with their smaller cousins, or that you can't let your dog off-leash while walking with him. I do it all the time with my hounds. They love going to the off-leash dog beach, playing at the lake, and hiking in the woods. However careful attention must be taken before releasing your hound, as many locations have strict leash laws. It's also imperative that you have spent time on basic obedience training in advance. If your dog won't come at home, then he certainly won't come when he has more interesting distractions.

As with all giant breeds, Irish Wolfhounds are just that: Giant. Their veterinary maintenance is higher, they will require larger toys, they will need more floor space than Lassie, and they definitely take up more room in the car. When I purchased my last vehicle, the salesman thought I was nuts when I whipped out my handy dandy tape measure and began to compare different SUV's based on how much room there was in the back with the rear seats down.

When grown, you'll find that your hound will spill over the edges of even a large dog bed, so you will either need a giant sized bed, a twin mattress, or two large dog beds placed side by side as I have in my car. (Yes, the one with the back seats down.) What's more, even though they are remarkably good at navigating around your furniture, you'll find that puppies can be quite clumsy and have a tendency to squeeze themselves into tight spaces they may have trouble backing out of. Oh, and let's not forget that long, rudder tail that can knock things off your coffee table.

If you're not watchful, this breed will wiggle his way into your heart before you realize it has happened. The IW is a dog that has an abundance of personality, but is also an intelligent animal that is relatively easy to train. They typically don't snap to orders faster than you can spit them out like a poodle, but you can almost see the wheels turning as they methodically obey your commands. They can be dopey and silly, playful and clownish, as well as refined and elegant. They tend to have a sensitive nature and truly want to please their human partners.

There is no question that an Irish Wolfhound can be an intimidating dog to a lot of people. I am commonly given a wide berth when I'm walking my hounds in a public area. However they generally make a better watch dog than a guard dog. A well socialized hound enjoys attention and will eagerly accept a pat and scratch behind the ear. Still, their size alone is usually a pretty good deterrent, and though they are a gentle breed, there are stories of them protecting their owners in desperate situations. After all, the official motto of the Irish Wolfhound is *"Gentle when stroked, Fierce when provoked."*

Another factor to consider is longevity. Sadly, giant dogs don't typically have as long a life expectancy as many of the smaller breeds. Generally, a hound that has made eight to ten years is considered to have had a long lifespan, though there are dogs that will have shorter lives as well as longer. The biggest threats to this breed are cancer, cardiac, and gastric dilation-volvulus syndrome (GDV), otherwise known as gastric torsion. If you decide to adopt an IW into your family, make sure the dog is from a reputable breeder. You want to be confident your dog has been bred from healthy lines, so that you and your companion can spend as many happy years together as possible. Don't be afraid to ask the breeder about the health of their dogs, and the longevity of their lines.

One other thing you will have to keep in mind is that the IW doesn't like hot temperatures. After all, they are Irish, and were originally bred for that environment. Depending on where you live, you may need to find ways to keep your dog cool during the summer months. Walk you hounds early in the morning or late in the evening, avoiding the hot hours of the day, and never feed your dog immediately before or after exercising. Some dogs really enjoy chomping on ice cubes, and you can make it fun for them by freezing special treats inside the ice. This is an especially helpful treat when your puppy is teething.

Make sure your dog has plenty of fresh water available at all times. Wolfhounds have a tendency to drink a lot of water, after which they seem to want a friendly snuggle with their favorite human, hence giving that person a shower from the dog's wet beard. Also, if possible, let your dog stay in an air conditioned area when it gets really hot. Many dogs also enjoy playing in the water sprinklers, so be inventive. Remember, if you're hot, then they almost certainly are, and on top of everything else, they are wearing a fur coat. And of course—as with all pets—never, never, never leave them in a hot car.

So in recap, if you're looking for a friend, the IW makes a great family companion. They love people and attention, and some are even used as therapy dogs. They are good with children and other pets, and are not overly energetic. In fact, they make pretty decent couch potatoes. Yet they are always ready to play when you are. As long as they get to stretch their legs a couple times a day, they are happy to sit around the house with you. Or if you want to go on a hike or jog down the beach, your IW will be right at your side. They are intelligent and easy to train, and really want to please their people. They usually like to play in water, though they do not typically enjoy swimming. Their grooming needs are generally simple as a rule. Keep their nails trimmed, their ears cleaned, and comb or strip out the dead hair. Even for the show ring, the grooming requirements are modest compared to other dogs. As one competitor said on a rainy show day, "We just knock the mud off before we go into the ring."

Chapter Two
History of the Breed

The Irish Wolfhound has been referred to by many names throughout history. In ancient times these dogs were frequently referred to as the Cu, as well as Irish Greyhounds, Celtic Greyhounds, and Irish Wolfdogs. They were also known as the Irish Hound and war dog. Today, many clubs and organizations still hold a gathering of the Cu, meaning the gathering of the hounds.

This ancient breed is certainly not a newcomer to the dog world, but rather has roots spreading back into the mysterious vapors of time. No one knows exactly when the origins of the breed began, but we do know from ancient carvings and writings that they existed at least as early as 273 BC, though there is evidence they were around long before that. After the Celts attacked the Delphi in 600 BC, a survivor left an account of the huge dogs who fought alongside their masters. Julius Caesar mentions them in his "Gallic Wars" writings, and Quintus Aurelius, the Roman Consul, wrote about the seven dogs that he received as a gift in 391 A.D. and "all Rome viewed with wonder."

The dogs are also mentioned in the old Irish laws, as well as in Irish literature. Probably one of the most famous stories took place at a palace in Beddgelert in 1210 AD. No one knows for sure if the tale is true or not, but it is embedded in Irish Folklore. Following is the account as depicted in "The Faithful Hound" published by Gwynedd Crafts, Beddgelert.

Gelert's Grave
In the 13ᵗʰ century, Llewelyn, Prince of North Wales, had a palace in Beddgelert. One day he went hunting without Gerlert "The Faithful Hound" who was unaccountably absent. On Llewelyn's return, the truant, stained and smeared with blood, joyfully sprang to meet his master. The prince, alarmed,

hastened to find his son, and saw the infant's cot empty, the bedclothes and floor covered with blood. The frantic father plunged his sword into the hound's side thinking it had killed his heir. The dog's dying yell was answered by a child's cry. Llewelyn searched and discovered his boy unharmed, but nearby lay the body of a mighty wolf which Gelert had slain. The prince, filled with remorse, is said never to have smiled again.

In addition to other skills, the Great Irish Hounds were used as war dogs, hauling men off their horses and out of chariots. Irish mythology is full of tales depicting their valiant bravery and ferocity in battle. As guard dogs, it was their duty to protect the herds and property. Of course, they were highly prized for their hunting skills, most notably for their ability to chase down and kill boar, Irish elk, which stood about six feet at the shoulder, and wolves. During the 1600's there were so many wolves in Ireland that the country was nicknamed "Wolf Land." That is where they eventually got their current name, Irish Wolfhound.

The dogs were held in such high esteem that only nobility could own one, consequently they were given as gifts to kings and emperors. It is said the chains and collars were often made out of precious metals and when disputes arose over the ownership of the dogs, full scale wars erupted. The number of hounds one was allowed to own depended on the person's position of status. Yet due to the heavy exportation of the dogs, and the fact that they hunted their prey out of existence (there are no more wolves in Ireland), the Great Irish Hounds nearly became extinct. A decree was issued in 1652 that prohibited the exportation of Irish Wolfhounds from Ireland.

Oliver Goldsmith wrote in his 1770 *Animated Nature,* "The last variety and most wonderful of all that I shall mention is the great Irish Wolfdog, that may be considered as the first of the canine species . . . bred up to the houses of the great . . . he is extremely beautiful and majestic in appearance, being the greatest of the dog kind to be seen in the world . . . they are now almost worn away and only very rarely to be met with."

The preservation of this gallant hound is credited to Captain George Augustus Graham, a Scottish officer in the British army. He collected the last remaining animals and in 1862 began a 23 year breeding program that brought the Irish Wolfhound back from the brink of disaster. It was under his supervision that the very first breed standard was established.

The Irish Wolfhound was officially recognized by the American Kennel Club in 1897 and is currently included in the hound group.

Chapter Three
American Kennel Club Breed Standard

The breed standard is the description of what the "ideal" or "perfect" specimen should look like. While no dog is flawless in every single detail, the standard is an invaluable tool for judges, breeders, exhibitors, and enthusiasts to use in order to identify the best representations of the breed. Without strict adherence to the standard, the breed would devolve and lose the qualities for which it is known. In short, the breed would change. While it is true the standard is open to a bit of interpretation, it is nevertheless an important guideline that must be followed in order to keep the breed true to its intended form.

The American Kennel Club
Official Standard of the Irish Wolfhound

General Appearance: Of great size and commanding appearance, the Irish Wolfhound is remarkable in combining power and swiftness with keen sight. The largest and tallest of the galloping hounds, in general type he is a rough-coated, Greyhound-like breed; very muscular, strong though gracefully built; movements easy and active; head and neck carried high, the tail carried with an upward sweep with a slight curve towards the extremity. The minimum height and weight of dogs should be 32 inches and 120 pounds; of bitches, 30 inches and 105 pounds; these to apply only to hounds over 18 months of age. Anything below this should be debarred from competition. Great *size,* including height at shoulder and proportionate length of body, is the desideratum to be aimed at, and it is desired to firmly establish a race that shall average from 32 to 34 inches in dogs, showing the requisite power, activity, courage and symmetry.

Head: Long, the frontal bones of the forehead very slightly raised and very little indentation between the eyes. *Skull*, not too broad. *Muzzle*, long and moderately pointed. *Ears*, small and Greyhound-like in carriage.

Neck: Rather long, very strong and muscular, well arched, without dewlap or loose skin about the throat.

Chest: Very deep. Breast, wide.

Back: Rather long than short. Loins arched.

Tail: Long and slightly curved, of moderate thickness, and well covered with hair.

Belly: Well drawn up.

Forequarters: Shoulders muscular, giving breadth of chest, set sloping. Elbows well under, neither turned inwards nor outwards.

Leg: Forearm muscular, and the whole leg strong and quite straight.

Hindquarters: Muscular thighs and second thigh long and strong as in the Greyhound, and hocks well let down and turning neither in nor out.

Feet: Moderately large and round, neither turned inwards nor outwards. Toes, well arched and closed. Nails, very strong and curved.

Hair: Rough and hard on body, legs and head; especially wiry and long over eyes and underjaw.

Color and Markings: The recognized colors are gray, brindle, red, black, pure white, fawn or any other color that appears in the Deerhound.

Faults: Too light or heavy a head, too highly arched frontal bone; large ears and hanging flat to the face; short neck; full dewlap; too narrow or too broad a chest; sunken or hollow or quite straight back; bent forelegs; overbent fetlocks; twisted feet; spreading toes; too curly a tail; weak hindquarters and a general want of muscle; too short in body. Lips or nose liver-colored or lacking pigmentation.

List of Points in Order of Merit

1. Typical. The Irish Wolfhound is a rough-coated Greyhound-like breed, the tallest of the coursing hounds and remarkable in combining power and swiftness.
2. Great size and commanding appearance.
3. Movements easy and active.
4. Head, long and level, carried high.
5. Forelegs, heavily boned, quite straight; elbows well set under.
6. Thighs long and muscular; second thighs, well muscled, stifles nicely bent.
7. Coat, rough and hard, especially wiry and long over eyes and under jaw.
8. Body, long, well-ribbed up, with ribs well sprung, and great breadth across hips.
9. Loins arched, belly well drawn up.
10. Ears, small, with Greyhound like carriage.
11. Feet, moderately large and round; toes, close, well arched.
12. Neck, long, well arched and very strong.
13. Chest, very deep, moderately broad.
14. Shoulders, muscular, set sloping.
15. Tail, long and slightly curved.
16. Eyes, dark.

Note – The above in no way alters the "Standard of Excellence," which must in all cases be rigidly adhered to; they simply give the various points in order of merit.

If in any case they appear at variance with Standard of Excellence, it is the latter which is correct.

Chapter Four
Prep Work Before Puppy Arrives

If you've decided to take the plunge and are bringing home an Irish Wolfhound puppy, then good for you. Your not-so-little bundle of joy will most certainly provide you and your family with lots of love and joy in the years to come. However there are some things you need to think about to get off on the right foot—or right paw—as the case may be.

Puppy Proof Your Home and Yard

Before you even consider bringing Puppy home, you need to make certain everything is ready for him (or her) in advance. One of the most important things you can do ahead of time is to puppy proof your home and yard. Remember, Puppy is just a baby and wants to learn about his new world in typical baby fashion. That means touch it, play with it, and most importantly, chew it. So here are a few tips on how to puppy proof your castle.

The best way to start is to think like a puppy. Get down on your hands and knees and look around your home from their vantage point. Puppies are curious creatures and will eventually want to investigate everything. Look for those power cords that are perfect for little teeth to chomp on, or that throw rug with the tassels on the end. Then there's that wonderful smelling trash can that just has to have something interesting in it, not to mention the—heaven forbid—poisonous plant sitting in the corner of the room.

You may think you have everything under control and that Puppy won't get into anything without you noticing, but it's easy to get distracted for a few seconds, and that's all it takes. Puppies are cute and clumsy, but it's amazing how fast they can go from playing with the chew toy you gave them to pawing open the cabinet door and lapping up toxic cleaners.

Keep in mind that if it's within reach, it's fair game. That includes things like your cell phone that's sitting on the coffee table, or the toilet paper hanging from the roll in the bathroom. And let's not forget the special jackpot bonus of the cat's litter box, or the nice smelly socks/shoes you left on your floor. Yummy!

The same is true for the outside yard. Please, please, please make sure it is securely fenced and that Puppy can't get stuck in, nor can he squeeze under, around, or through the posts or gate. Also remember there are plants, such as oleanders, that are toxic. If you're not sure whether some of your landscaping is safe, please contact your veterinarian.

I would also suggest you don't let your new buddy hang out in the garage because of the potential chemicals he could get into. For example, anti-freeze is sweet tasting and dogs love to drink it. Unfortunately the primary ingredient, ethylene glycol, is highly toxic and will send them into the big doghouse in the sky if they do.

So go ahead and take the time to look at the world from your puppy's point of view before he arrives. A few preventative measures now may very well save you from losing your favorite decorative pillow, or worse, a trip to the vet's office.

Get All Your Paperwork in Order

You should get an information/care packet from your breeder before, or at least when, you pick up your new friend. Included in that packet should be your puppy's sales contract and transfer of ownership/registration materials. (Or proof that the papers are pending with the appropriate kennel club—which is the American Kennel Club if you are in the United States.) You should also receive the medical records showing when Puppy was vaccinated and wormed, as well as any other vet check-ups he may have had. Some breeders will even have your puppy micro-chipped in which case you will need to register the chip number with the appropriate organization and/or the AKC so that if Puppy ever does get lost he can find his way back to you.

Another item you should have in your packet is your puppy care instruction sheet. I would ask for this sheet **before** you pick up your puppy so you can already have the appropriate food at home. Some breeders will give you a copy ahead of time, as well as include a copy in your information/care packet. This form will give you the breeder's recommended feeding schedule, and inform you as to what Puppy has already been eating. Furthermore, the breeder should send home a sample of the puppy's regular food. It is important that you don't change your pup's diet right away. He will be stressed enough with leaving his home, mom, and littermates. If you are planning on feeding him something other than what the breeder suggests, then please change the diet slowly after Puppy has had a chance to settle into his new environment. Refer to Chapter 5 for more information on how to feed your Irish Wolfhound.

Notify Your Veterinarian of the New Arrival

Your breeder should have had a wellness checkup done by a veterinarian prior to you picking up or receiving your new puppy. Many breeders will also require you to have your veterinarian conduct another wellness checkup within a few days after you get Puppy. It is typically stated right in the sales contract. This is done for the protection of all parties involved.

As the buyer, you want to make sure your puppy is healthy before you bring him home. Of course, the seller will want to verify the puppy is still in good health after he arrives to his new home. It will also allow your veterinarian to begin a chart on your new friend, and to advise you when you need to worm and vaccinate your dog in the future. To that end, it is recommended that you contact your veterinarian in advance once you have confirmed the date Puppy is coming home and make an appointment for a couple days after your new puppy arrives.

Appropriate Toys
What's In Your Toy Box?

There are a ton of dog toys available on the market today. Some of them are really good, while others are only fit for the trash can. Some toys may be great for a Yorkshire Terrier or Pomeranian, but not well suited for a Neapolitan Mastiff. In order to keep your hound happy and safe, there are several things you need to think about before buying that cute stuffed animal on the shelf.

First off, the Irish Wolfhound is a giant breed of dog. Giant breeds have giant mouths—go figure. So when you're selecting a toy for your dog, you need to make sure it's large enough that your hound can't choke on it. Also keep in mind that your puppy will grow very fast, so even though the chew toy you gave him on his way home from the breeder is fine today, next month it may be too small. Always keep tabs on the condition of anything you give your hound to play with, and replace it as necessary.

Another important thing when choosing a toy for your pal is that IW's have very powerful jaws. After all, they were bred to kill wolves by snapping their necks. While your new puppy won't have the bite force of an adult dog, it is still wise to remember that they are stronger than you might think. Never select a toy that can be crunched into smaller pieces, or that has parts—such as eyes—that can be chewed off and ingested.

Any toy that can fray apart, like most rope toys, are also a bad choice for an IW. I heard about one dog that chewed a rope until it frayed, and then swallowed the pieces. It caused an impaction that had to be surgically removed.

I would also caution against bones, antlers, or other such objects. Some of them have sharp edges and can damage your hound. Not to mention that some dogs have had their teeth chipped or broken from chomping on bones.

Not all toys are bad though. One good choice, especially for a chew happy puppy, would be a size appropriate Kong, which can also be filled with treats. Similarly, Nylabone makes some good chew bones that are appropriate for Irish Wolfhounds. Another trick that my hounds love is an empty 2 liter soda bottle. Just make sure you remove the label wrap and the lid so they can't choke on it. The bottles make a fun crunching sound when the hounds chew them.

Some stuffless toys are also a favorite, so long as they don't have eyes, ears, or noses that can be chewed off and swallowed. My puppies love stuffless toys. Just monitor the toy and take it away or replace it as needed, and as with anything else, use common sense when selecting Puppy's next play thing.

The Versatile Exercise Pen Known as the X-Pen

You will need to have a crate for Puppy to sleep in, and a place for him to call his own. While sometimes a puppy will be shipped to you in an enclosed crate, you will find your baby will not fit in it for long. Thus, you will need something that will continue to work as your pup grows up into adulthood. The exercise pen, more commonly referred to as the x-pen, is a perfect solution. The x-pen is also ideal for keeping your hound out of trouble, for traveling, and for housebreaking. (See crate training for detailed information.)

Chapter Five
Bringing Home Your Puppy

Picking Up Your New Bundle of Joy

The big day is here, and you are finally bringing Puppy home to stay. It's an exciting time, and everyone is elated. Naturally you'll want to show off your new family member to your friends and family, and fuss over the new arrival. However let's back up and think about this from the puppy's point of view.

For you it's a day to play, but for Puppy it's a day of stress. He will be leaving everything he ever knew: his home, his mother, and his littermates. Everything will look, sound, and smell different, and he won't understand why. The best thing you can do for Puppy is to keep things quiet for a few days and help him become comfortable with his new surroundings.

Try to plan Puppy's arrival for when you will be home at least a couple of days. Make sure it's not a busy day around your house. Bringing home a puppy for Christmas or other high energy event is not a good plan. Things will be stressful enough for your new baby, and you don't want to add to the tension. If you keep things quiet, you'll find most puppies will adapt very quickly to their new home.

A few items you will want to have packed in your puppy bag are an appropriate sized nylon collar (NEVER put a choke chain on a puppy), leash, chew toy—which will save your fingers from being gnawed—and towels. Your breeder should also give you your puppy packet, which was discussed in Chapter 4. If at all possible, get a towel or toy that has the mother's scent on it. Most breeders will be all too happy to rub a cloth you brought along over the mother if they don't already have something prepared. It will be a comforting smell to your new friend, and can help him settle.

Your puppy may or may not be accustomed to wearing a collar, but if you have to stop on the way home you don't want him getting away from you and running into the street. Make sure the collar is tight enough it won't easily slip over the ears, but not so tight that it will be restrictive or uncomfortable. It's also a good idea to have a couple towels handy just in case baby face gets car sick.

If you are picking up your puppy by yourself, you will want to keep him in a crate as you travel. It would be dangerous for Puppy to be crawling over your lap and jumping down around your feet while you drive. I put a seatbelt around the crate and have it turned so the door is facing me. That way the puppy can see me and know that he isn't alone. Be careful to keep the temperature of the car comfortable for the puppy, even if it means you are a bit too warm or cool. Also, avoid having vents blow directly on the puppy.

If you are picking up your youngster with a friend, then have whoever is handling the pup for the ride home sit in the back seat with a towel draped over their lap in case the puppy springs-a-leak or gets sick. It is very tempting to sit in the front with the puppy, but that's not a good idea. It's very easy to get distracted while driving if the baby is right next to you, plus there won't be any room to set the puppy on the seat if needed. Remember, by the time you bring your new puppy home, he will probably weigh over twenty pounds.

In the event that you have a fairly long travel time, you will also want to pack some water and a bowl. Be cautious giving Puppy anything to eat until you get home since he could get car sick. If you do decide to give the puppy something, make sure it is a kibble he is already used to, and only give a few pieces at a time. If your travel time is measured in days rather than hours, by all means feed the pup on his regular schedule. Just be aware that it's possible you will be revisiting his meal if he gets sick. If you are on a windy road, it is advised to wait until the road straightens out before feeding, since curvy roads tend to aggravate a nauseous stomach.

Also be aware that puppies need to relieve themselves on a frequent basis. As a rule, they can typically hold it for about two hours if they are two months old, three hours if they are three months old, and so on. If Puppy starts crying and squirming, and it's been a while since your last bathroom break, he may be saying he needs to "use the grass." Make certain you stop someplace safe and never open **any** car doors until the puppy handler says they have a firm grip on the hound, and that the puppy is properly leashed. You will also want to choose an area that has not had other dogs on it, since Puppy has not completed his baby shots yet, thus he is not well protected from contagious diseases, such as Parvo. Also, please be a courteous owner and have plastic bags—or necessary bags—to pick up any solid waste Puppy may leave behind.

We're Home—Now What?
Low Key: The Key to Happiness

You're home at last with the newest member of your family, so what happens next? Before you even bring your hound inside the house, it's a good idea to take him to whatever area you have designated as the "relief" area. It may be necessary to give him a few minutes, and when he begins to go, say whatever command you wish to use for the cue. This should be the command you give him from now on when you want him to do his thing, so make sure you choose something that won't embarrass you when/if you need to use it in public. Many people use the phrase, "Go potty." When Puppy finishes his business, praise him profusely.

Though you may want to introduce Puppy to the other animal inhabitants of your home, as well as the neighbors, friends, and family, as mentioned above it's best to give your hound some quiet time. He will probably want to sleep a lot since his is still a baby, and he has a lot of growing to do. So please resist the temptation to wake up your puppy to play, and teach your children to respect Puppy's nap times. There will be plenty of time to play with him when he wakes up on his own.

You should already have an exercise pen (x-pen) set up in the main part of the house, yet away from the constant flow of traffic. In fact, I keep two pens set up. One in the living room, and one in my bedroom. The x-pen will be the equivalent of your puppy's bedroom, or from his point of view, his den. Make sure it is not in a drafty location. He will need soft blankets or a bed in his pen, a toy, and a water dish. A stainless steel water pail with a handle is a wonderful choice. It works great when you use a swivel eye lobster clasp to clip the handle to the x-pen so the pail doesn't tip or fall over. Your puppy needs to be inside this pen anytime you are not eyes-on, hands-on with him. It will keep him safe, and he will be less likely to have an accident as dogs are clean animals and do not like to soil their dens.

The best thing you can do now is to start his regular routine right away. Just keep things low key until he's had a chance to adapt to you and his new home. The more interruptions on the normal flow of family life, the longer it will take for your hound to settle in. However, puppies are amazing creatures and you'll find if given the chance, it doesn't take them long to feel like part of the family.

Despite how adorable and cuddly your puppy may appear, he is not a teddy bear. Please be careful with how you allow your hound to cuddle. What might be cute for a puppy now, may not be so endearing with a fully grown dog. Never allow your puppy to do anything you don't want a mature dog to do. That includes things like jumping up on you, or on the furniture if he won't be allowed to later, and respecting that you are the pack leader.

As with all babies, your puppy will probably throw a bit of a ruckus when he doesn't get what he wants. Being his leader, it is imperative that you don't give in to Puppy's demands. Of course, you have to be kind and loving to your new buddy, but there are times you have to put your "paw" down. A perfect example of this will probably occur the first night.

Most puppies will feel insecure and lonely the first few nights at a new home. This usually translates into whimpering and crying. It is your responsibility to not give in to the puppy and go cuddle him to make him feel better. This will only cause an abundance of problems down the road. Instead, you need to invest in a pair of ear plugs, ignore his cries, and sooner or later he will go to sleep. That being said, remember that puppies need to relieve themselves often. You will be up several times a night taking Puppy outside for the first couple of months. If Puppy is restless and crying, and it's been a while since his last bathroom break, then by all means take him out. While he's doing his business, give him the command you will use from now on, and then praise him when he's done. Do not let him play or you will simply teach him to cry to get his way. Then take him back inside and return him to his x-pen or crate. Most puppies cease their crying in a week or so if you don't give in to them. You may feel sorry for Puppy at first, but in the end you'll be glad you were strong, and so will your puppy.

Feeding: The First Couple Weeks

Your puppy's breeder should have given you an information sheet that outlines what, and how often, Puppy has been eating. At a young age, puppies should have four meals a day. Whatever you do, do not change his food for at least the first several days, and better yet, for the first couple of weeks. Then if you do decide to change his food, do so gradually. You don't want to upset your puppy's digestive track.

Introducing Puppy to Other Pets

It's best to allow your puppy a couple days before introducing him to your other pets. Be aware that if you already have other pets, they will consider the house their domain, and the puppy will be the intruder. Only let the pup meet one other pet at a time, and keep a watchful eye. You don't want your new puppy to become frightened or hurt, nor do you want your other pets injured. IW puppies can be rather clumsy at times. Often, it is easiest to allow the meet-and-greet to happen while Puppy is in his x-pen. That way they can see and smell each other, but are still protected.

If the other pet is a dog, then let the current dog smell Puppy's tail first. For dogs, this is akin to shaking hands for a human.

Try to keep everything as low energy as possible. Don't forget that Irish Wolfhounds are sighthounds and still have a strong prey drive. It is instinctive for them to chase other animals. They must be taught that your other furry family members are not prey, but rather their new best friends.

Do not let your puppy play unsupervised with any other pet until you are confident that both the puppy and the other animals will conduct themselves appropriately. This may take a little time, so don't rush it. However, it's best if they don't play unsupervised for several months in case the activity level becomes too rough.

Chapter Six
What's On the Menu?

Do I Look Fat to You?

Before getting too deep into how to feed your Irish Wolfhound, a note should be made regarding what your IW should look like. This is a galloping hound, like the Greyhound, Afghan, and Borzoi. They are not a draft breed, nor should they look like one. Contrary to popular belief, a roly poly puppy is not necessarily a healthy one. You can actually cause joint and bone issues if your dog is overweight, and pushing your puppy to grow as big as possible as fast as possible severely increases the risk of developmental bone disease.

So how do I know if my dog is at a good weight? A quick way to determine if your hound needs to join Weight Watchers, or would benefit from adding a couple more pounds is to feel his ribs. There should be a slight amount of fat around them, yet you should easily be able to feel each distinct rib—just not the Grand Canyon. On the other hand, if you have to press to get your finger between the ribs, then it's time to cut the calories. The same is true for the shoulders, spine, and hips. You should be able to feel a tad of flesh around them, but it shouldn't feel like a Jell-O bowl either.

Another indicator is does the dog have a waist, and an abdominal tuck. (This is less noticeable in young puppies.) The IW is a deep chested breed, and the area behind the ribs should be smaller in diameter than the chest. If your dog doesn't have a well-defined tuck-up, then he's overweight.

How to Feed Your Irish Wolfhound

All dogs need a high quality, well balanced diet, and that is especially true for the giant breeds. They grow incredibly fast and it is important to provide adequate nutrition while keeping the risk of developmental bone disease at a minimum. With a new puppy, you should continue to feed whatever he is used to for a couple weeks, even if it is a less than perfect food. You can then gradually switch Puppy over to his new menu if you feel a change is necessary. The below information should help you make that determination.

Naturally you will want to make sure your little hound has fresh water available at all times. It's amazing how much these guys drink, so keep an eye on it less they run out.

You will also want to spread out Puppy's meals throughout the day. In order to keep your hound from becoming a finicky eater, you will want to feed each meal at regular times every day. Give your puppy twenty minutes to finish his meal, and if he doesn't, then take it away until the next scheduled feeding time. Do not leave the food out free choice, nor wait an hour and try to get him to finish up. This will only create a picky eater that you don't want to have to deal with later. If the puppy consistently leaves a little food behind, then reduce how much you give him. If he finishes up quickly and is looking for more, go ahead and feed him a little more in the next meals—as long as the pup is not getting too heavy. It is better for Puppy to be a *tad* underweight than overweight. Also, spread the meals out to equal times throughout the day. You don't want to go twelve hours overnight, then feed every three hours during the day. Below is the recommended number of meals your dog needs according to age.

Puppies 3 months to 6 months = 4 meals a day
Puppies 6 months to 10 months = 3 meals a day
Puppies 10 months and older = 2 meals a day

Never feed an IW of any age less than two meals per day to help avoid gastric torsion. Please do not exercise your hound for two hours after a meal, or one hour before a meal.

This can also lead to gastric torsion, which may kill your dog. More information on this subject in Chapter 10: Health Care.

You may find that some active hounds are more difficult to keep weight on than those who are less energetic. If that is the case, you may need to go back to three meals per day. I typically don't like to feed more than three cups per meal if I can avoid it.

If you are feeding a good, quality food, then there is no need for additional supplements. Most certainly DO NOT feed your puppy calcium supplements. This is dangerous to his bone growth and can permanently damage your dog.

There has been a lot of debate over the years regarding the regulation of protein in a growing hound's diet. It was believed that too much protein would contribute to the risk of joint and bone disorders, however that is not the case. Current research shows there is no evidence to link high protein intake to skeletal disease in large breeds. Instead, the causes include genetics, overfeeding, over exercising at too early an age, and excessive calcium in the diet.

Below are suggestions and guidelines of what to look for in a quality food for an IW. Most of these suggestions are true for any breed as well. You will find that higher quality feeds have fewer fillers—such as corn—and are better metabolized by your dog. This means you won't have to feed quite as much bulk, and you won't have as much waste to pick up off the lawn. Also, be aware that the percentages posted on the label are frequently the minimum amount in the feed, and can potentially be higher than stated.

- Top ingredients should be meat based. They should be name *specific* such as beef, lamb, chicken, etc. 'Meal' is acceptable, (such as beef meal), and is actually a more concentrated source of protein since it's already dehydrated and thus has less water weight.
- Avoid generic, or *non-specific* meats such as meat meal, poultry meal, etc. Fish is not considered specific, unless it states what kind of fish, such as salmon.
- Avoid too many fillers such as corn, and if there are fillers, they should not be the main ingredients.

- Protein should be 24 to 26%
- Be extremely cautious of the calcium to phosphorus ratio. If there is too much calcium it can lead to your hound growing too quickly. This is known to cause permanent joint and bone disorders. The calcium to phosphorus ratio should be around 1.1:1 (1.1 to 1) and **absolutely** no more than 1.5:1.
- Avoid any foods that contain dye. Don't just go by the visible color of the food. It's common to see dyes such as Red #40 and caramel coloring.
- Look for glucosamine and chondroitin sulfate in the list of ingredients if your hound is over a year of age. These are natural compounds manufactured by the body. Glucosamine is believed to aid in the formation and repair of cartilage and chondroitin is believed to promote elasticity and inhibit enzymes that break down cartilage.

- Look for soy free. Soy can cause gas, thus increases the risk of bloat.

Be cautious with assuming a dog food is superior because it is expensive and/or well known. Just because it says "Premium" on the bag, doesn't make it a quality food. There are many elite brands out there that I would never give to my hound. Also, while there are some good puppy foods available, be diligent and inspect the list of ingredients as many do not pass the quality test. In a lot of cases, an All Life Stages food is better. Remember that many puppy foods are specifically formulated to encourage rapid growth, which is something to be avoided in the slower maturing giant breeds.

You can add a little yogurt to the diet, but make certain it is plain with no sugar added. This is easily digested and has beneficial bacteria that aid in digestion.

A lot of people like to give their dogs table scraps as a treat. Some will argue human food is terrible for dogs and should never be fed, while others do not feel there is an issue if a few precautions are met. I will feed table scraps to my dogs, but they are never fed as the main meal. They are reserved for treats. Do not go overboard on human food since you do not want your dog to start turning his nose up at his regular dog food. You also must be careful what you permit your dog to have. Cooked bones are brittle and very hazardous. They can cause internal perforations and potentially kill your dog. Other foods that are toxic and on the no-no list are items such as chocolate, grapes, onions, and garlic.

However, one really good treat your hound can have is ice cubes. Some dogs and puppies really enjoy munching on them, and since ice is nothing more than frozen water, it is a healthy treat to provide. Especially on those really hot days.

Another treat dogs really love is peanut butter. Put some inside a Kong and freeze it. The dogs enjoy licking it out, and it gives them mental stimulation at the same time. You can also freeze a little peanut butter inside an ice cube. Note: ice cube—not ice block. You don't want to hurt your dog's teeth with the iceberg that sank the Titanic.

One type of feeding that is popular in certain circles is the homemade raw diet. While a lot of owners feed this menu plan successfully, I would highly advise against it unless you are a canine nutritionist or are well versed with the dietary needs of your hound. Too many people think dogs are carnivores, while in fact they are omnivores with strong carnivore tendencies. If a raw diet is fed, special consideration must be made to ensure the dog has the appropriate balance of vitamins and minerals. Otherwise your dog will be missing nutrients he needs, and his health can suffer. That does not mean I never give my dogs raw meat. However I only give it as a treat—such as the fat trimming off my steak before I cook it, or a small piece of raw hamburger meat—and the dog must be on a regular worming schedule, which should be done regardless of the diet.

Chapter Seven

To Exercise or Not to Exercise:
That Is the Question

Despite their giant size, the Irish Wolfhound does not require a giant amount of exercise. In fact, you will want to keep your hound's exercise routine fairly limited as a young puppy. Too much stress on puppy legs can cause joint issues later. As the dog grows and matures, he will be able to do more activities.

Two Months to Six Months

For the first six months or so of your new puppy's life, you'll want to keep his activity level pretty low key. Of course he will need to play in order for his muscles to strengthen and develop, just don't let him play in a yard that is not properly fenced. Also, bear in mind that unlike some of the smaller breeds, IW's are still growing and developing until they are at least eighteen months old, though they should pretty much be treated as a puppy until they are around two years of age. Just as humans, some puppies will develop faster than others. Their legs and joints are particularly vulnerable to damage and injury due to their rapid growth rate. Thus, in order to protect your youngster's health, be extremely mindful of the items listed below.

- Don't let your puppy play with other dogs without supervision. Even if your puppy knows or lives with the other dogs, rough play is bound to end in injury.
- Never allow your puppy to go up and down stairs, nor jump off of things such as the sofa, a bed, and most certainly not out of the car. You need to keep the impact on his joints to a minimum.

- Don't let your puppy walk across slippery surfaces such as linoleum, laminate floors, tile, etc. He can easily lose his footing and do the Bambi routine, which can have dire consequences. Giant breed dogs are especially susceptible to this type of potential injury.
- Never encourage your puppy to make sudden turns, or quick stops. Again, avoid any impact or abrupt stress on those joints.
- Do not expect your puppy to go on walks with you until he is around six months old—and even then on a limited basis. This does not mean you can't work on leash training, just don't expect your hound to walk more than five or ten minutes. However your pup will enjoy free exercise with you in a securely fenced area. Just remember what we said about those sharp turns and rapid stops. Don't do it. ☺
- Start working on basic obedience training, such as leash training, sit, down, come, stay, etc. Keep your sessions short. Several five minute sessions a day are better than one thirty minute session.
- If your puppy gets tired, by all means let him sleep. He has a lot of growing to do. They grow so fast, sometimes I think they are bigger when they wake up then they were when they fell asleep.
- Socializing a young pup is very important, but do not allow your puppy to go anyplace where another dog may have been until he finishes his puppy vaccines. You don't want your baby to contract a disease such as parvo which can be fatal.

Six Months to Nine Months

- Start taking Puppy for short walks on the leash. Most pups will be able to safely walk around one half to one mile. Start with short walks, and gradually increase the distance.
- If your puppy gets tired or doesn't want to walk that far, shorten the distance until he matures a little more. Don't push him at this age.

- If you have to go up and down steps, make sure Puppy does so at a controlled walk. No running or jumping. This will be true for the rest of his life. If traveling, get a hotel room on the ground floor if possible, and if not, take the elevator. The IW is longer than he is tall, and a flight of stairs can be difficult. However, it is always best to keep stairs at a minimum. More about this later.
- Your puppy may look like a dog by now, and he is certainly bigger than most dog breeds by this age, but he is still just a puppy. Continue to monitor how rough your hound plays with other dogs. While activity is good for him, overzealous play can still damage his developing joints.

Nine Months to a Year

- Gradually lengthen your daily walks. By the time your puppy is a year old, you should be able to walk a couple miles.
- Your puppy will also enjoy some free running in open areas if you have any available. However, be cautious where you allow your hound off-leash. Sighthound—remember? They love to chase things.

Over a Year

- Once your puppy is a year old, you can begin to exercise him as if he were an adult. You can also start lure coursing if you—and more importantly, your hound—are interested. Just be advised to watch him, as some hounds do mature faster than others. If he shows any signs of limping, stiffness, or just seems like he's a little off, take a break for a couple days. Otherwise, go have a ball with your hound.

Chapter Eight
Training: Key to a Happy Relationship

Understanding Dog Psychology

One of the most common mistakes people make when dealing with animals is to anthropomorphize them. (Ascribing them human characteristics, behavioral and thought patterns.) Humans are very unique creatures, and we tend to let our emotions dictate our actions. For example, if someone makes us angry, we may want revenge or carry a grudge against that person. We might do something unkind to *get even*, or secretly rejoice when things don't go well for our *not-so-favorite* individual. Lucky for us, dogs aren't like that.

Unlike humans, dogs live in the moment and don't think about what happened last month, last week, or even last night. Contrary to what some people believe, our canine friends don't destroy the house while you're gone because they didn't get a share of that juicy steak you had for dinner last night. They don't chew your favorite rug because they're mad at you for yelling at them to stop barking, and they don't have "accidents" in the house because they are getting back at you for making them get off your bed. The mind of a dog simply doesn't work that way. It never has, and it never will. To effectively train a dog, you need to know how his mind *does* work.

To start with, dogs are pack animals. Regardless of the breed, all dogs are canines and originated from animals that probably looked a lot like a wolf. In the social world of dogs, there is an Alpha, or pack leader, who lays down the rules and tells everyone else what to do, and when to do it. When your dog was still with its mother, she controlled such things as eating, sleeping, and playing, and she disciplined the puppies that didn't follow her rules. Now that your puppy is no longer with his mother, he will be looking for who will play the role of top dog. If you don't immediately assume that role, then Puppy might take over since dogs are uncomfortable when they don't have an established dominance order.

Once that happens, you will not effectively be able to train your dog, because in his mind, he is the leader, and you should do what he says. This is where so many behavioral problems arise from, and why so many dogs are given away or taken to shelters. It's not the dog's fault—he's simply confused and insecure because to him, there is no order in life. Thus, from the very beginning you need to establish that you are Alpha of your pack, and that you set the rules. If there are multiple humans in the family, then the dog must understand that he is last man on the totem pole. Believe it or not, your dog will be more confident and happy if he understands that you are the leader of your doggie pack.

This means you need to have rules that Puppy must follow, and if he breaks the rules, he needs to be disciplined. Now this doesn't mean that you abuse your dog, screech at him like a sick peacock, or hit him—which you should **never** do— but you will have to let your dog know he did something you dislike. Typically this is done by reprimanding Puppy in a firm voice, then showing him what is acceptable. For instance, you catch Puppy chewing up your eight hundred dollar rug and you feel a wave of anger overwhelm you. It is your job to maintain control and say "Leave it," or "Off"—whatever command you choose to use as long as you're consistent—in a calm yet firm voice, then offer your dog something he is allowed to chew such as a Nylabone. When he takes the appropriate toy and begins chewing it, praise the dog like he just won the Nobel Prize. You just established you are the rule maker, and you saved your rug in the process by showing Puppy what he is allowed to chomp on.

Just like humans, all dogs have their own individual personalities. Some canines will be more motivated to perform for a treat reward, some by getting to play with a specific toy for a minute, while others are more praise orientated. It is up to you to learn your dog's traits, and to help him as best you can. There are trainers who are against food rewards, but if that is what best motivates your dog, then use it to your advantage. Once the dog has learned the desired behavior, you can gradually wean him off the toy or treat reward, but still praise him for his effort. For example, if you ask for a sit and he responds consistently, then skip the toy/food reward every once in a while, only offering praise. As time goes on, skip the toy/treat every third time, then every other, then only give it occasionally, but don't forget to tell him he was a good boy for doing what was asked of him.

So in recap, you will need to make sure of the following before starting your training regimen.

- Immediately establish yourself as pack leader.
- Don't be afraid to discipline your dog, but always do so in a non-abusive, non-emotional manner. Be firm, but kind.
- Dogs live in the moment. Never reprimand *King Patrick* unless you catch him in the act of misbehaving.
- If at all possible, redirect the undesired behavior with something that is desired, such as chewing a chew toy instead of your furniture.
- Make sure your dog has the proper nutrition for his age, breed, and/or circumstances.
- Learn what motivates your particular dog and use that to your advantage.
- Make sure your dog has enough daily exercise for his age, and/or personality. Just don't overdo the activity level with a puppy.

Leaving Puppy Home Alone

This topic is a big concern for a lot of dog owners. We don't want our dog to be scared, sad, or lonely when we leave, so being the compassionate owners that we are, we tend to cuddle the pup (or dog) saying things like, "It's okay baby, I'll be home soon," or "Be a good doggie while I'm gone." Raise your hand if you've ever done this. (Yes, I raised my hand too.) Well guess what, you just set your dog up for emotional distress and failure. Dogs are excellent at reading body language and energy levels. You projected to your best buddy that you are upset, telling him that something is wrong. No wonder he has problems with your departure.

The best way to teach your puppy—or adult dog—is to practice in stages. Keep the energy level low, and don't make a production out of your departure. Simply put the puppy wherever he will be when you're away—let's say a securely fenced area in your backyard. Make sure to leave a chew toy with him as well. Don't baby talk him or act like you're sad that you're leaving. This puts you in a weak position in his eyes, and will cause stress. Leave him in his area and walk away out of sight. Then after a few seconds, return if he's still quite. If your puppy starts to get agitated and cry, do not return until he's settled and quiet. This will only teach the puppy that if he cries you will come running. It will also sabotage other training down the road. Continue doing this, increasing the amount of time that you are away.

Some dogs will be comforted if you leave a radio or the television on while you're absent. Any background noise that is familiar and that he associates with you and/or the family being present.

Crate Training
The Den is Our Friend

Is putting a puppy (or dog) in a crate and locking the door the same thing as putting him in doggie prison? Is it cruel and inhumane? Well in truth, the answer is both yes and no. Yes, it is cruel if you expect the puppy to stay in his crate for hours and hours while you go to work. Not to mention the fact that his bladder won't let him stay in that long without a bathroom break. It's also true that it is inhumane if you are using the crate as a form of punishment. However, you'll find your puppy will love his crate and will treat it as his personal bedroom if you use it correctly.

There are many benefits to having a puppy that is crate trained. One of the best perks is that it's the fastest and easiest way to house train them. It also comes in handy during travel, if the puppy is looking for a nice quiet place to nap, you need to limit his access to the house, or if Puppy wants a safe retreat when that thunderstorm frightens him.

In the wild, a dog's home is his den. Crate training simply uses this natural instinct. However you do need to make sure the den you provide is the right size. While some of the plastic flight kennels are fine for shipping an eight week old puppy, they are unsuitable for him as he grows. (Which he will do very quickly.) To know if the crate fits the dog, ask yourself if the dog can comfortably stand and turn around, lay down and stretch out, and sit. Considering how large IW's get, I have found it best to use a collapsible exercise pen, or x-pen. The 36" tall ones are fine, even for an adult hound. They have folding panels, so you don't have to open it to its maximum capacity while your puppy is still young. Just make sure to secure the folded panels together so the pup can't wiggle his way between them and injure himself. The x-pen is also very portable, which makes it ideal for you and your hound if you travel.

There are a lot of instructions out there on how to crate train your puppy or dog, and though informative, I differ somewhat since I use an x-pen rather than an enclosed crate. I have used the following method for years with my IW's and have never had a problem. In fact, my dogs love their x-pens.

With a young puppy that has not been house trained, I will frequently lay a plastic liner under the pen, then place comfy blankets on top. He should have free access to water, but make sure the pail is clipped to the pen to prevent it from tipping over. The pen should be opened up enough for the puppy to move around, be relaxed, and lay down, but not so much that he will want to use a corner as a bathroom. Dogs don't like to soil their sleeping and eating areas, so they will try to keep from having accidents in the pen unless they can't hold it anymore. (Which would be your fault for not taking him outside.) You should also have a chew toy inside for him to play with.

When you first introduce your puppy to his x-pen, set him inside, offer him a treat, and tell him what a good boy he is. Let him explore his new surroundings, and if possible, put in a cloth that has his mom's scent on it. You will also want to feed

Puppy his meals inside the pen. I try not to leave him alone, and will sit next to the pen until he's comfortable. Then open the door and tell him what a great Puppy he is while you head for his outdoor potty area. (Puppies need to go a lot.)

When you do leave him alone, do so for short periods of time, then come right back. Frequently I will wait until he has fallen asleep, then I'll go sit on the sofa. When he wakes up, he can still see me, but I'm not right next to him. Then if he's quiet for a couple minutes, I'll go get him for a bathroom break and praise him. If he starts to whine, ignore him until he's quiet, unless he paws the sides of the pen. If he does, sharply say "No," then go back to ignoring him until he's quiet. Gradually increase the amount of time Puppy is in the pen without you next to him, then slowly work on leaving the room. Most puppies will adapt very quickly to their x-pen as long as you remember he doesn't live in it. You still need to let your pup out for people time and play time. When he's tired, let him retire to his pen and take a nap.

House Training

House training your puppy typically isn't that hard, but it does require you to pay attention. As mentioned several times already, small puppies spring leaks on a regular basis, and it's up to you to know when to take him outside. First and foremost, if your pup has an accident inside the house, it was probably your fault for not paying enough attention. And unless you physically catch Puppy "in the act," do not reprimand him. He's just a baby and doesn't know any better. Instead, you need to teach him where he's supposed to do his thing.

So when will Puppy need to use the facilities? Pretty much count him needing to go after the following occurrences:

- Eating and/or drinking. Feed Puppy at the same time every day. Not only is it better for his digestive health, it will make it easier to predict when he will need to go outside. As soon as he finishes eating, take him outside. (Yes, even if he just went half an hour ago.)

- Waking up. When he is still very young, you will need to pick Puppy up and carry him outside as he will undoubtedly spring that leak before getting to the door if you let him walk.
- Playing—especially after (or commonly during) rigorous play.
- A two month puppy can generally only hold it for about two hours, a three month puppy for three hours (Less often if playing, as noted above.)

Always keep an eye on Puppy, and be mindful that he may need to go at any time, whether you're expecting it or not. Also be aware he may not give you a lot of clues he's about to water your carpet, but there are some signs you need to be conscious of that will save you from buying another bottle of carpet cleaner. (And when you do clean your carpet, make sure you use a cleaner that is recommended for pets. One that will not only remove the stain, but also the scent so Puppy doesn't smell it and try to return to the same area again.)

One sign that your puppy is about to have an accident is if he starts sniffing the floor in an unusual manner—especially if he's making circles. Puppy may also start walking a little stiff and hold his tail in a funny position. When you see these behaviors, you know you don't have much time. Get Puppy outside. Though it's best if you got him outside before he started looking around for a place to go. You should be taking him out on a regular schedule so you don't have issues.

Having said that, there is the classic puppy behavior of simply squatting down with no advance warning, even if he was in the middle of doing something else first. If that happens, sharply say "NO," then immediately scoop Puppy up and take him to his designated relief area outside.

When you do take Puppy outside, make sure it doesn't turn into play time. You are there for one purpose, and one purpose only. Put your puppy on a leash, even if he isn't leash trained yet. You can follow him around his bathroom area as needed, just don't let him leave the relief area until after he has completed his business. When he starts to go, give him the verbal command that you have decided on, such as "Go potty." Keep saying it until he finishes, then praise him enthusiastically and give him a treat. He will learn to associate the command with the act, so eventually you will be able to get him to go when you ask him to. Very handy when traveling.

When Puppy makes a mistake and you didn't witness it, there is nothing you can do except clean it up. Whatever you do, don't take your pup over to the mess and then yell at him, and certainly don't rub his nose in it. He won't understand what he did wrong, and all you're likely to accomplish is to make the puppy afraid. If he's nervous or frightened, he'll probably make the same mistake again.

Socializing

One of the most essential things you can do for your puppy is to properly socialize him. He needs it for his mental health, and to feel confident and comfortable in the world around him. It will also teach him what is, and what is not, appropriate behavior around people, as well as other dogs. This is of paramount importance considering how large your puppy will eventually grow to be. Dogs that are not socialized are much more likely to react in fear at unfamiliar sights, sounds, and situations, whereas dogs that are socialized are less stressed and live happier lives. Studies have shown that to reap the best benefits of socialization, it needs to be done while the puppy is still young. The socialization your puppy receives up to the age of twelve weeks is the most critical. A reputable breeder will have already started the socializing process with your puppy by exposing him to many different things, but once you bring Puppy home, the rest is up to you.

Before you go gung-ho and rush your puppy off to the nearest dog park, remember that he has not received all his vaccinations yet. Until that time, you will want to keep him away from any location that has, or has had, any dogs on it. Socializing your puppy is a wonderful thing, but it won't seem like it was a great idea when he comes down with a life threatening disease that could have been avoided. Your breeder and your vet can help you with when it's appropriate to start taking Puppy to public locations.

However, there are things you can do for him in the meantime. Get him used to being touched and handled everywhere, including his ears, and between the pads of his paws. Roll him over on his side and back, and get him used to you looking at his teeth. This type of desensitizing will really assist you when you take him to the vet. This is also fantastic bonding time for you and your canine buddy.

It's also great to have friends and neighbors come play with Puppy. Just don't invite anyone over who has dogs that aren't fully vaccinated. If you know anyone with children, or someone who has a beard, get them to come visit. The same is true for an elderly person, or someone who uses a wheelchair or walker. Wear funny hats around the puppy, make strange noises, show him different types of ground such as concrete, asphalt, grass, dirt, etc. In short, pretty much anything you can think of that's different. Even opening and closing an umbrella. Just be careful to introduce things slowly. You don't want to frighten Puppy. That can cause more harm than good. If he's nervous or fearful of something, back off and let him approach it on his own terms. Go sit by the object and when Puppy comes up to you, offer him a treat. Just take it easy until he shows you he's not afraid.

Once his puppy shots are completed, you can start taking him on outings. Let him hear and see new things and interact with strangers. I even go out of my way to a specific dog park that is near the train tracks. There is also a playground and a skateboard park next door, so it's an opportunity for the hounds to hear and see things they wouldn't ordinarily be exposed to.

Puppy obedience classes are another wonderful tool in your socialization arsenal. You can accomplish multiple tasks at once by attending these classes. Not only are you socializing your pup, but you will be working on teaching him things all dogs should know such as sit, stay, down, come, and heel. And again, your hound will be thrilled to be spending time with you. If you socialize your puppy, and teach him to listen to your commands, there is no limit to the fun the two of you can have.

Please read the last chapter, Have Fun with Your Hound, for some ideas of the activities you and your best friend can do together.

Chapter Nine
Grooming

The Irish Wolfhound does not require a great deal of grooming, though I would suggest going over him a couple times a week with a metal comb. You will also want to clean his ears, and pluck out any hair that is growing inside the canal. Using blunt-ended scissors, trim the longer hair under the tail, and on the sheath of males. This will help him stay cleaner when he relieves himself. You can also trim the hair around the feet so it doesn't look like he's wearing slippers. Make sure the leg hair blends down into the trimmed area on the paw so it doesn't look cut. Thinning shears work well for this.

Clip the nails regularly, but only take a little at a time so you don't cut into the quick. If you do accidently cut too deep, styptic powder can be applied to stop any bleeding. However, cutting too deep is painful and your hound will soon learn to jerk away, making it nearly impossible, and dangerous, to do his nails.

For a tidy appearance, keep the hair on his head stripped, using your forefinger and thumb, to the point where you can see the shape of the skull. You don't want him to look pulled, just cleaned up. Also strip the longer hair on the ear leather, leaving behind the very short hair that feels like velvet. You can also use a stripping knife for this. Using thinning shears, carefully trim back and blend in the ridge of hair that forms a "V" on his neck— affectionately referred to as a cobra neck. Also tidy up the area around his cheek, but never remove any of his beard or eyebrow.

His bottom line should have a definite tuck-up appearance, so carefully strip the longer guard hairs under his flank area. Any tufts of hair sticking out by themselves should also be stripped, no matter where it is on the body.

The base of the tail, known as the dock, will sometimes look like there is a thick ball of hair around it. This ball can be fixed and blended by gently striping out the longer hairs. Likewise, if longer hairs are hanging down the length of the tail causing a flag effect, pull out the longer hairs, or use thinning shears.

There is no need to bathe the IW on a frequent basis. In fact, if you do it can soften his wire coat. Basically only bathe him if he gets dirty, and use a shampoo designed for wire hair coats.

Puppy coats require very little care, but it's good to get into the routine of grooming maintenance now, even if you just go through the motions. It will teach the hound to hold still while you give him his salon treatment.

When your puppy is around seven months old, you will notice that the longer hairs will start to pull out fairly easily. At this point, it is recommended that you hand strip your pup. As with the ears, using your forefinger and thumb, gently pull out the loose hairs, taking only a few hairs at a time. (Some prefer to work with a stripping knife, but be careful not to break hairs. You want to remove them, not cut them.) Work in small sections, and don't try to do the entire coat in one sitting. This generally takes a little time and your puppy will probably get tired of it. However the end result is worth the effort.

Right off the bat your pup's color will be more vibrant and crisp because you removed the dead hair. Moreover, when the coat grows back in it will be appear healthier and have more of a wire texture to it, as opposed to a duller color and a soft feel. If you ever plan on showing Puppy, this is a step I would not skip.

Chapter Ten
Health Care

Naturally the goal of every Irish Wolfhound owner is to keep our hounds as healthy as possible. In order to accomplish that goal, we need to take preventative measures and know how to recognize when something goes wrong. Below are some important measures we can take to protect our noble friends.

Have Your Veterinarian's Contact Number in All Your Directories

Hopefully the occasion will never arise that you have a medical emergency, but in the event that it does, you may not have time to look around for your vet's contact information. Have your veterinarian's name, phone number, and address listed in all of your telephone directories. (This includes the contact information of a good 24 hour pet emergency clinic, in case your dog needs help when your regular vet's office is closed.) You should have the numbers in your personal phone book that resides next to your house's base line telephone. If you don't have a personal book, then at least have a business card holder near your phone with your veterinarians' business cards in it. This is not only handy for you, but also for anyone else that may need quick access to medical care for your dog. If someone is taking care of your dog while you are away, make sure your caregiver knows exactly where the numbers are.

You should also have this information recorded in your cell phone's contact list, if you have a cell phone. Additionally, it is advisable to keep a copy of both vet's business cards in your wallet. It's better to be over prepared and have these numbers in multiple locations, than it is to need the numbers and not have them available. Your dog's life may depend on quick action from you one day.

Name Collar and Microchipping

What if your dog ever gets lost? You may say that will never happen, and that your dog will always come back to you. However, what happens if he spots Peter Rabbit and he takes off after him, or your yard's gate is accidently left open and your dog wanders off? You'll want to be able to find your precious friend quickly, and with as little stress as possible. This can be done by having a properly adjusted, flat nylon collar on your dog at all times. Imprinted directly on the collar is your dog's name, and your phone number. That way if he's found by another party, they can reach you easily. There are many pet stores, including online, that sell such collars. You can also get them in a vast array of colors in case your hound is a fashion diva. I have a different color for each of my dogs.

But what if the name collar comes off? If your dog is taken to an animal control center, or is taken into a vet's office, the first thing they will do is scan the dog for a microchip. If found, all your contact information will be readily available to the office. Microchipping is also advised in case you ever need to prove the dog actually belongs to you. Furthermore, it's not a bad idea to have a current photo of your canine buddy, and not just a cute head picture. A full body picture—or conformation picture—is best.

Vaccinations and Worming

Keeping to a vaccination and worming schedule is an important step to maintaining your dog's health. While it is true some feel the vaccines and wormers do more harm than good, the risk of your dog contracting a deadly disease such as Parvo is far, far higher. Yes, there are occasional incidences where an animal has had an adverse reaction to an inoculation, yet in the thirty years I've owned dogs of multiple breeds, I've never had one that had a problem with a properly administered wormer or vaccine. Be advised I said properly administered, as some breeds are more sensitive to certain medications than others. For example, Collies are known to have issues with ivermectin, which is the drug used to protect dogs against heartworm.

Also remember that in the US, vaccinating for rabies is required by law after your pup reaches 4 months of age. Below is the Humane Society's recommended vaccination schedule, as well as a list of the diseases, and what they are.

Humane Society Recommended Vaccination Schedule

Puppies: **
6-8 weeks: first shots = DHLPP + Corona
11-12 weeks: second shots = DHLPP + Corona
15-16 weeks: third shots = DHLPP + Corona
4 months: Rabies (repeat in 1 year)
Start on Heartworm prevention (for life)

Adults: **
DHLPP: yearly
Rabies: every 3 years after first year booster
Bordetella (Kennel Cough): 1 or 2 a year.
> Note: It is highly recommend every six months if the dog will be exposed to other dogs, or be in places other dogs have been, such as a dog park. Also note many dog boarding facilities will not accept a dog that is not current on all vaccines, including Bordetella.

** Please talk with your vet regarding their recommended de-worming schedule and flea/tick control for your area.

Description of Diseases

The **DHLPP** vaccine listed above is for **D**istemper, **H**epatitis, **L**eptospirosis, **P**arainfluenza, and **P**arvovirus.

Distemper: Canine distemper is a serious airborne viral illness of the lungs, intestines, spinal cord and brain that has no known cure. The disease affects not only dogs but can be carried by several common species of wildlife including raccoons and skunks as well as pet ferrets.

Hepatitis: Infectious canine hepatitis is a contagious viral disease spread by body fluids of infected dogs, wolves, coyotes, fox, and bears causing an acute liver infection which can be fatal.

Leptospirosis: A group of bacteria causing liver and kidney disease that is spread by the urine of affected animals including rats, pigs, raccoons, skunks, and cattle. The bacteria can remain active in the soil for up to six months and often makes its way into water sources such as puddles and ponds where your dog may be exposed by drinking the water.

Parainfluenza: Canine influenza (originally from horses) is a highly contagious flu-like virus causing an upper respiratory infection (bronchitis) that can be mistaken for kennel cough but is much more serious and potentially fatal.

Parvovirus: Parvo (Canine parvovirus) is a highly contagious potentially fatal viral disease that starts in the intestines but also attacks the white blood cells, and when young animals are infected and survive, the virus can damage the heart muscle producing lifelong cardiac problems.

Corona: Canine Coronavirus (CCV) is a highly contagious intestinal disease that can be found in dogs all around the world; the most common source of infection is exposure to feces from an infected dog, especially at places and events where dogs gather.

Rabies: Rabies is a severe, and often fatal, disease that affects the brain and central nervous system. The virus is transmitted through the saliva of an infected animal, either by a bite or when infected saliva makes contact with mucous membranes or an open fresh wound of another animal or human. The main carriers in the U.S. are foxes, raccoons, skunks, and bats.

Bordetella: Also known as Kennel Cough, Bordetella is an upper airway bacterial or viral infection that is spread through the air or on contaminated surfaces making dogs most at risk when visiting public areas such as events, dog parks, or kennels.

Please note that vaccinations take a couple of weeks before they are effective, and your new puppy should be considered at risk until he has completed his entire puppy series of 3 doses—some veterinarians recommend 4 on giant breeds—of DHLPP.

I would advise you keep a record of what vaccines your dog has had, and when he is due for a booster. Many veterinarians will send out reminders for you, but it is best that you have a backup reminder for yourself. In addition to keeping up to date on vaccines, you will also need to keep your dog current on worming medications, including heartworm. Also, don't forget to keep your dog protected against tapeworm. A number of wormer medications do not target the tapeworm, so be sure to ask your veterinarian.

Spay or Neuter

Unless you plan on showing your hound in the conformation show ring, or plan on breeding your dog, it is best to have him (or her) neutered or spayed, as the case may be. Please remember that breeding should not be taken lightly, and only animals that will help contribute to and improve the breed, should ever be allowed to reproduce. Most reputable breeders will have an agreement in the sales contract to have your puppy sterilized, unless other arrangements have been specifically agreed upon in advance.

There has been a lot of debate over what age to sterilize your dog, ranging from just a few weeks up to a couple of years. Most proponents of waiting until the animal is older stem from the belief that the odds of developing bone cancer or cardiac disease are lower. While there are studies that tend to lean in this direction, there are also studies that rebut the assumption. One must also remember that giant breed dogs are more prone to these conditions anyway.

The general rule of thumb in the dog world is to have your pet sterilized before they reach six months. This is largely to keep them from ever being able to reproduce. Most dog breeds are reaching their sexual maturity around this age. However, giant breeds such as the IW develop at a much slower pace than smaller breeds, and frequently do not reach sexual maturity until around a year. (Or longer in many cases. It just depends on the individual.) It is not uncommon for a bitch to be well over a year old before coming into her first heat. Even so, it is recommended to spay or neuter the dogs around one year of age.

I have found over the years that some people tend to have more trouble with neutering their dog than spaying their bitch. Yet males will be under less stress if they don't have those raging reproductive hormones surging every time he's around, or even smells, a bitch in heat. And they can smell it from quite a distance. You might need to invest in a good pair of earplugs because IW's have big lungs and can howl with the best of them. If you don't live a good distance from your neighbors, be assured your neighbors will not be very happy with you as your intact male serenades the females. The males may also get restless, go off their food to the point where they lose weight, and will find it difficult to pay attention. He will be looking to escape and find a way to his potential mate, so you have to be extra careful with your fences and gates. If there are other males around it can break out into a fight, and one or both of the dogs could wind up seriously injured if not dead. (Also, never try to physically break up a fight with dogs of this size lest you wind up in the hospital yourself.) The dog will not turn back into the relaxed guy you know for anywhere from several days to three weeks, depending on the pheromones the bitch is releasing. Even after the bitch no longer accepts a breeding from a male, she still smells good to him, so time is not on your side. This is not a two or three day deal.

Likewise, when the bitch goes into heat, she will typically get restless, and can also go off her food. She will bleed for days if not weeks, and her vulva under her tail will become swollen. This can get very messy, both on her own coat as well as your carpet. It is imperative to keep her far away from males during this time, though she may not agree with this decision. Again, you have to be extra careful with fences and gates, and it's best to keep her indoors as much as possible. Not only to prevent a pregnancy, but also to be kind to any males that may be in the area. The duration of the heat cycle will vary from bitch to bitch, but it's not uncommon to take three weeks from start to finish during which time you will not be welcome at dog parks, social events, or places where other dogs might be, even if she is on a leash.

Having your dog and/or bitch *fixed* will not only save you from a lot of headaches, but your hounds will be spared the hardships of the heat cycles. How often your bitch will come into heat will vary greatly between individuals. I've had hounds that would cycle every four months, though that is pretty short for a dog of this size. But unless you have a really good reason for breeding, have researched the bloodlines to make an informed match, have carefully considered the good attributes as well as the faults of the dog and bitch, are willing to have a potentially enormous vet bill—especially if a cesarean section is required—and are willing to keep and care for any puppies which you are unable to find suitable homes for, then please have your hound altered. It will save you and your buddy a lot of grief.

Hygromas: False Bursa

A hygroma—or false bursa—is a non-painful swelling that forms a pocket under the skin. It can occur over the bony protrusions of the elbow, hock, or hip of the dog, though it is most commonly found on the outside of the elbow. Hygromas are initially small, but over time can grow to be a couple inches or more.

Hygromas are caused by repeated trauma or pressure to a joint—such as laying or sitting on hard floors or surfaces. In order to protect itself, the body forms a fluid sac around the area. This is seen frequently in puppies, because they tend to throw themselves to the ground harder than adults. Though unsightly, the best treatment for a hygoma is to leave it alone, and simply correct the situation that is causing it in the first place.

If you take your dog or puppy to the vet, do not let him/her aspirate the fluid. This is generally not effective, and can just open the area up to infection. Instead, you will want to have soft beds strategically placed where your hound likes to camp out. Orthopedic foam beds work well, as do twin sized mattresses. Basically anything that is soft, yet thick enough to relieve the pressure from the joint when your hound is sitting or lying down. It may take some time but if properly protected, most if not all of the hygroma will be reabsorbed.

Because the IW is such a large dog, he should have soft, comfy beds his entire life to protect his joints, starting from puppyhood. After all, how would you like to sleep on concrete? I have beds in my living room, bedroom, back porch, and inside the back of my car. (Yup, the same one I discussed in the beginning of this book.) I also bring the car beds into the hotel room with me when I'm traveling. Pretty much, my hounds will always have access to a soft place to lay down no matter where we go.

Longevity

Large breed dogs do not typically have as long of a lifespan as do the smaller breeds. With the Irish Wolfhound, if a dog lives to be eight to ten years old, he is considered to have had a full and long life. Most will say the average life span is between six and eight years, though when searching for a puppy to bring into your household, I would encourage you to ask about the longevity of the parents' lines.

Remember that average means just that—there will be individuals that live shorter lives, and of course there will be those that live longer lives. I know of some IW lines that are averaging around six years, while I know of other lines that are averaging around ten years.

I have heard many people say they would love to have an IW, but are afraid to because their short life span will break your heart. Again, while it is true they won't be around in twenty years like your toy poodle might be, the actual life span of a few other breeds might surprise you. Some breeds that you may know that have a similar life span as the IW include: Bulldog, Bernese Mountain Dog, Boxer, Bull Mastiff, Chesapeake Bay Retriever, Chow Chow, Great Dane, Greyhound, Mastiff, and Saint Bernard.

Osteosarcoma

Osteosarcoma is the most common form of bone tumor found in dogs. It is an extremely aggressive cancer that spreads quickly, and has a tendency to extend into other parts of the dog's body. This is known as metastasis, which is defined as the transference of disease-producing organisms or of malignant cells to other parts of the body by way of the blood or lymphatic vessels or membranous surfaces. The giant dog breeds are at the greatest risk for osteosarcoma.

Unfortunately, current medical knowledge does not completely understand the causes of these tumors. However some symptoms include: lameness, joint pain, lethargy, and swelling. To diagnose osteosarcoma, the veterinarian will frequently take several X-rays from different angles. Other techniques include blood tests, bone scans, and biopsies. Once osteosarcoma has been confirmed, the prognosis of the dog is not good. Chemotherapy is often used to treat the tumors, though sometimes amputation of the limb is performed.

If your dog is diagnosed with osteosarcoma, careful pain and care management will be required. In some cases, you may consider euthanizing the dog. As difficult as that is, there are cases where it is more humane to the dog than to ask it to try and live in constant pain. Currently there are no known measures that can be taken to prevent the tumors.

Heart Disease

Heart disease is one of the leading health concerns for giant breed dogs. There are many different types of heart disease, such as congestive heart failure (the heart is not able to pump out blood as fast as it is comes in causing a backup or congestion of body fluids), myocardial disease (the heart muscle weakens causing it to enlarge) and congenital defects (which are present at birth), just to name a few. Regardless of the type of heart disease, you should seek the assistance of a veterinarian.

There are some warning signs to be aware of that are indicative of heart disease. Again, if you notice any of the below symptoms, you should immediately consult your vet. Also, be aware that just because your dog exhibits one or more of these symptoms does not mean he has a heart problem. There are other conditions that may have similar indicators. Likewise, a few of these indicators may simply be normal behavior for your dog. Yet when in doubt, don't risk the health of your best friend.

Here are some warning signs of heart disease.

- Cough
- Difficulty Breathing: This includes shortness of breath and labored or rapid breathing. Do not confuse this with normal panting. Dogs are unable to sweat except on the pads of their feet and their nose. Thus, in order to cool the body down, they exchange heat through the process of panting.
- Lethargy: The dog is less playful than normal, or is he wanting to isolate himself when that is not his typical behavior. Also look for general weakness, and reluctance or intolerance, to exercise.
- Loss of Appetite: It's not uncommon for a dog to go off his food for a meal or two—or longer if your dog is anywhere near a bitch in heat, or you have a bitch who is in heat. However, if it is persistent, there may be a problem that needs to be addressed.
- Restlessness: Your dog may be seem uneasy or anxious.
- Edema: This is the swelling of body tissues, especially in the abdomen and extremities.
- Chewing Feet: Since the feet are the farthest part of the dog from his heart, they will sometimes swell just like what happens in humans. Note that dogs will sometimes chew their feet when they have cardiac issues or are uncomfortable.

Again, not all of these symptoms will mean that your dog has a heart problem. There may be other health concerns that need to be addressed. However, your vet can run tests to see what the problems are and address them appropriately.

Gastric Dilatation-Volvulus (GDV)

Gastric Dilatation-Volvulus, otherwise known as gastric torsion and twisted stomach, is a life threatening condition common to deep-chested breeds such as the Irish Setter,

German Shepherd Dog, Weimaraner, Great Dane, and of course, the Irish Wolfhound. This condition is known to cause death within hours, so it's vital to seek immediate veterinary care if your dog develops the disorder.

Frequently GDV is incorrectly referred to as bloat. Bloat is when the stomach fills with air, and/or food and fluid. The distended stomach puts pressure on internal tissues and can cause difficulty breathing, as well as reducing the blood supply to other organs.

GDV can start with bloat then progress to this life threatening condition. Because the stomach in many deep-chested breeds is free-floating, in certain conditions it can literally twist, or rotate around its axis, thus causing a blockage. (Think of a severely kinked water hose.) The consequences of the torsion include emergency situations such as progressive distension of the stomach, increased pressure in the abdomen, damage to the cardiovascular system, as well as decreased perfusion (the pumping of blood into organs or tissues). Inadequate perfusion can lead to cellular damage and organ death. The symptoms of GDV include the following:

- Distended abdomen
- Anxious behavior
- Depression
- Abdominal pain
- Unsuccessful attempt to vomit or belch—dry heaving
- Weakness
- Shortness of breath
- Excessive salivation
- Rapid heartbeat and/or weak pulse
- Pale gums
- Collapse

The exact causes of GDV are currently unknown. However, there are certain risk factors which are included below.

- Eating too much in one meal. It is important to split your adult dog's food into at least two meals per day, and puppies

between three and four meals per day, depending on age. Please refer to chapter 6.
- Eating too quickly, or gulping food
- Overeating
- Stress
- Eating before or after exercise. Do not allow your hound to physically exert himself—this includes rough play—until two hours after eating, and don't feed him until one hour after exercise.

If your dog shows any symptoms of bloat or worse, GDV, call your vet immediately and tell them you are bringing in a possible gastric torsion case. Then get your dog to the vet's office as quickly as you safely can. GDV can kill a dog very quickly. If the stomach has indeed rotated, emergency surgery may be required. Even with prompt medical attention, the dog may not be able to be saved. Remember, time is of the essence.

Should I Let My Dog Stand Up On His Hind Legs?

If you have ever seen an Irish Wolfhound stand up on his hind legs, it is truly an amazing sight. This breed can stand up to seven feet tall when rearing up, and a lot of people are impressed with the sheer size and magnificence of the dog when doing so. However, there are some problems with allowing your dog—or worse—teaching your dog this behavior.

First of all, standing up on their hind legs is hard on the dog's back and hind end. Even if you are supporting his front feet on your shoulders, it should not be encouraged. In fact, I strongly advise that your dog never be allowed to do this behavior. Not only for his own health, but potentially for the health of others.

If your dog feels that it's okay to jump up and put his paws on your shoulders, then it must be okay to do so with anyone. Right? (Think about this from the dog's point of view, not yours.) Now what happens when an elderly person, disabled person, or simply an unsuspecting person enters the equation? Your IW thinks it is a fun game and up he goes—then down goes the person when they are knocked over by the enormous weight and power of your dog. There are people that could wind up in the hospital. I have relatives that could easily break bones such as legs and even a back if an animal the size of an IW pushed them over. Or what about a child or someone who is already intimidated by the dog? This action certainly does not make your dog a good ambassador for the breed, and will only serve to instill more fear of dogs from the victim. Not to mention that once the individual hits the dirt, the hound will most likely swamp the person, thinking play time is getting more interesting.

Not long ago, I was at an Irish Wolfhound event where one of the exhibitors had taught his hound to jump up. The handler was a young man, probably in his late teens, and didn't normally have a problem holding the dog's weight in such a manner. Unfortunately the dog became overly excited and in an effort to feel secure, performed a behavior that usually got him praise and affection. In this case, the handler wasn't expecting it and lost his balance and control of his dog. The dog, not understanding the problem, became even more assertive in trying to jump up, resulting in the handler's chest being deeply scratched by the dog's front claws. The handler very nearly lost the dog's leash in the outburst, and did successfully upset several other hounds and handlers that were in the immediate vicinity.

The moral of the story: do yourself a favor and don't teach your dog to jump up. It's physically not good for your dog, and can seriously injure a person, even if they *are* expecting it.

The Dreaded Stairs

As discussed earlier, stairs are not necessarily an IW's friend. As a youngster, they can cause all sorts of leg and joint problems, and as an adult, they can do the same if not navigated properly. If stairs are unavoidable, please make sure your hound takes them slowly and thoughtfully. Stairs put a lot of stress on a hound's legs—especially going down—and care must be taken to avoid injury.

That being said, I purposely teach my dog's to traverse steps so they are familiar with them. However, I always keep the dog on a short leash, and will pause at the top and bottom of the steps during training so the dog never learns to rush them. Additionally, I only use a short span, such as the steps up the front porch, the small section of six to eight steps found in some parks, or the downtown area of some cities. Never use a full flight of stairs if you can at all avoid it. Especially if the back of the steps are open so you can see through them. This will frighten many dogs, and it can be catastrophic if your dog has a panic attack halfway up or down, and if a leg slips through the open area at the back of the stair. If this happens, you could have a broken leg on your hands, or worse. Please use the elevator when you must go upstairs, as all public places are required to have handicap access. If you are traveling with your dog and stop at a hotel, request a ground floor room. It will make it easier taking your dog out to use the facilities anyway.

No Bones about It

There's no doubt about it—dog's love to chew bones. The problem is, as mentioned in chapters 4 and 6, bones can be a hazard. They can have sharp edges that may cut or poke, and they are very hard. There are dogs that have chipped or broken teeth gnawing on bones. If the bone is small enough to be ingested, or a piece breaks off that is swallowed, it can cause a perforation in your dog's stomach or bowel. This is potentially a life threatening situation. I have known dog's that have pierced their bowels from less obtrusive objects than bones.

If you insist that your dog have a bone, then please make certain it is still raw, and not a cooked bone. Once cooked, they become brittle and much more dangerous to the health of your dog. This is also true of chicken bones. Under no circumstance is a chicken bone, or that of any fowl, appropriate for your dog. The only type I would consider is a long bone which can be purchased at a butcher store or sometimes in the meat section of some grocery stores. However, I still recommend staying away from bones and antlers. There are lots of safe chew toys available to satisfy your dog's love—and need—to chew.

Elevated Food Bowl

Another controversial topic is whether deep-chested breeds should have their food bowl elevated. Some advocate that elevating the food bowl only serves to increase the occurrence of bloat and GDV. Others insist that elevating the bowl decreases the risk. I have seen studies done by clinics and veterinarians that conclude they do, and they do not, raise the incidence of GDV. So what are we to conclude is best for our hounds? To answer that, we have to remember there are other considerations to keep in mind regarding GDV.

First off, the speed in which the dog gobbles his food has been found to increase the risk of bloat and of gastric torsion. If you have a real chow hound at home, then find a way to slow his eating down. I have used a food bowl with pegs in it that worked really well. The dog had to eat around the pegs, which slowed her consumption time considerably.

Another important factor is exercise. Remember to never allow your hound to exercise or play rough for an hour before eating, or two hours after eating so that he is never exercising with a full stomach nor filling his stomach until he is completely recovered.

If there is a lot of corn or other fermenting material in the food you give your dog, then that can cause gas expansion in the dog's stomach, thus leading to bloat. It can also potentially lead to GDV as well. When feeding dry kibble, which I do a lot of, and the dog drinks a lot of water before or after eating, it can cause the dry food to expand in the stomach. Some feeds are worse than others. Run a test yourself by placing a small amount of dry food in a bowl and soak it in water. Notice how much the food swells. The same thing will happen in your dog's stomach. The feed that overly swells is not as good for the dog as the kibble that doesn't swell as much.

So you can see, there are other factors that must be taken into consideration when stating whether the food bowl elevation has anything to do with the occurrence of GDV. Personally, with a dog the size of the Irish Wolfhound, I suggest elevating the bowl to the height of the dog's elbow. It is also easier for them to reach and is less stressful on their front end.

There are several ways to raise the bowl. My favorite is an elevated feeder with an airtight storage compartment underneath. Some will accommodate a forty pound bag of kibble in the storage area, making storage and feeding a snap. However, these raised bowls will be too tall for a young puppy. For the youngsters, the cheapest and easiest solution I have found is to use a cardboard box of the right height. Simply cut out a circle in the box so that your food bowl will fit in, but the rim will not fall through. As your puppy grows, you can get a new box, until he reaches a height where he can use a more permanent structure.

Chapter Eleven
Having Fun with Your Hound

There are so many fun activities you can participate in with your well socialized hound. I recommend signing your puppy up for obedience classes once he's fully vaccinated. These classes are fun for both humans and dogs, and are a great way to get a head start on your basic commands. They are also wonderful tools for socializing your pup with new experiences as well as other dogs, and for bonding with your new best friend. Just make sure to choose a reputable trainer before signing up.

Once your puppy is leash trained and vaccinated, the possibilities of what you and your hound can do together are nearly limitless. My hounds adore going to our favorite dog beach where they can run and play in the surf and meet new people. They also love going to the dog park, heading out to the lake, hiking on mountain trails, and even simply going for a walk at home. Anytime they can be with you is happy time for an IW, and if the activity is something different or new, so much the better. Just remember that most public places have a leash law in effect, and never ask your puppy or dog to do something he's not ready for physically or mentally.

Another great idea is to join an IW club. Most clubs will have multiple events you can participate in every year. This is a fabulous way to spend time with your dog, but also other people who have the same love of the IW as you do.

Some IW clubs will have what's known as a Cu—a gathering of the hounds—at least once a year. They may have informal classes that discuss grooming, handling, and showing your dog. They may even have conformation show ring classes you can enter, though no points are awarded toward an AKC championship. A lot of people will also bring their puppies to the Cu as an introduction to traveling and showing. Because this is an informal event, there is no pressure on you or your hound to perform. Sometimes there will be a small lure course set that even puppies can run, and a CGC test may be offered. (See below for information on lure coursing and CGC.) All in all, it's a fun time for everyone, including the dogs.

You can also help the club represent our ancient and majestic breed at various events such as parades. We participate in the St. Patrick's Day parade every year with our dogs, who just eat up the attention they get from the crowds of people.

Some clubs are also invited to participate in fairs, such as a Celtic Fair. These events are an entertaining way to share our dogs with the public, talk about their history, and show off their wonderful dispositions, often while wearing period costumes.

I would also recommend practicing for, and taking a CGC test, or Canine Good Citizen. In the past, this was presented as an award, but effective January 1, 2013 the CGC became an official title that can appear on an AKC registered dog's papers. (King Patrick will become King Patrick, CGC.) The test includes ten various obedience and socializing skills, something your dog should know anyway. These tests are offered at many AKC shows, and sometimes at an IW club's Cu. For detailed information on the test and the skills needed to pass, visit the AKC's website at www.akc.org.

If you have a dog that really likes to run and chase things, you may want to consider trying your hand at lure coursing. Your hound must be a year old to be eligible to compete. In lure coursing, the sighthounds chase artificial lures—which typically look like white trash compactor bags—around a field meant to simulate coursing live prey. A typical lure course is around 600 to 1000 meters long.

Rally obedience is another popular way to show your dog, though it's also a blast to simply practice at home and have a good time. If you wish to show your dog in the conformation ring, the animal must be unaltered, however that is not true for the other competitions. In an obedience class, you must wait for instructions from the judge. However in rally, the competitor goes around a course of designated stations, with each station sporting a sign of what the competitor is supposed to do. There are usually anywhere from ten to twenty stations. The dog must be in a heel position unless otherwise instructed by a sign. Unlike obedience, competitors are allowed to encourage their dogs along the way. If you are interested in rally, I would suggest you go to an AKC dog show and watch other competitors. The same suggestion holds true if you are interested in obedience, agility, or any other event. You can also obtain information on specifics by visiting the AKC website.

No matter if you decide to show your dog or not, the most important thing is to include him as a member of the family and spend time with him. Some dogs thrive on a show life, whereas others do not enjoy it. Please do not force your dog to engage in an activity that he doesn't like to do. Your hound wants to be your best friend, and as long as you treat him that way, he will shower you with love and devotion for his entire life.

Congratulations on choosing an Irish Wolfhound to be your loving companion!

No matter what activities you decide to do with your hound, just have FUN and ENJOY him.

Made in United States
Orlando, FL
30 August 2022